I dedicate this book to all members of my family, especially my dear Mother and Father

Sue Denvir

Devon Days

To Marion

By Sue Denvir

with Love on Mother's
Day March 1996.

from
Audrey xxx

First published in Great Britain in 1994

Copyright © Sue Denvir

ORCHARD
PUBLICATIONS

2 Orchard Close, Chudleigh, Newton Abbot, Devon TQ13 0LR
Telephone: (0626) 852714

British Library Cataloguing in Publication Data
CIP Catalogue Record for this book is available from the British Library

ISBN 1 898964 06 8

Designed, Typeset and Printed for Orchard Publications by
Swift Print
2 High Street
Dawlish
Devon EX7 9HP

1

Devon Days

Devon Days

Sue Denvir,
Née Carter

The creative work in this book relates to my life in Devon since the 1920s, covering events and customs which are now part of history – a way of life which has disappeared for ever.

I grew up on a small dairy farm, the eldest of seven, four brothers and three sisters. Life was hard, money scarce but in spite of this we were, and still are, a happy and united family.

I have always loved the country, taking great pleasure from just being a part of it, in all seasons and all weathers. Animals figure largely in my life and like most country people I have great respect for animals that come under my care.

In the old days the City of Exeter held a special place in the hearts of young and old alike, as it was there that we met regularly on market days and on Saturdays to follow our various pursuits as I have described in, *'Saturday Night.'*

In our own little village there was always something going on. We were all part of a caring community, helping out on Fête Days, Christmas and other events often to do with the Village Church. Much of what I have written is now part of our cultural heritage, which hopefully will rekindle memories for older people as well as enlighten younger readers on our way of life in the not so distant past.

Westcott Farm, Rockbeare

Milking the Cows.

When I was twelve my Father said,
"It's time you learnt to milk the cows".
I grabbed a bucket and a stool
Then to the shippen, learning rules.

"I'll give you Daisy to begin,
For she is quiet and stands quite still.
Put your bucket and stool just there".
With that I sat, and said a prayer.

There stood Daisy chewing her cud,
All nonchalant and good as gold.
I took her teats, all soft as silk
and squeezed them gently – till the milk

Came trickling down all rich and warm
Into the bucket, some over the floor.
"Well done", said father, full of praise
You can come on down here right away.

"We'll call you up – be here at seven,
To milk out Daisy, Snow and Bluebell,
If you shape up well, then I'll be free
To give up milking – just suits me".

From that day on at seven and five
In the shippen rain or fine
To milk the cows became my lot
Whether I wanted to or not.

Our Devon herd was twenty-four
Milking took an hour or more,
And being me – a 'girt darned fule'
I was wedded to the milking stool.

The Driving Lesson.

"Come my dear, I've harnessed Joey,
He's waiting in the milk-run cart,
I'm going to teach you how to drive
Jump up front – let's make a start".

"If you can drive you'll come in useful
To take the milk to Rosamund Ford.
I'll be freed for other work
It'll suit me fine – upon my word".

He drove the cart at break-neck speed,
Past the post box – then he slowed,
Stopping there we both changed places,
I was to drive along the road.

"Now hold the reins, keep them slack.
A slack rein's what controls a horse".
I pulled the right rein a might too hard
We finished up in neighbour's yard.

"You silly girl – look what you've done,
Pull the left rein – straighten out!"
I tugged the left and father shouted,
I'd overdone it without a doubt.

He'd had enough of teaching me,
"You numb-skull, cant you show more gump?
Give me the reins and sit this side".
Then he drove home, all in a hump.

I was laughing up my sleeve
To beat the old man was such fun.
He'd caught me on the milking lark
But on the milk-run I had won.

Rosamund Ford. Local milk depot for the neighbouring farms.

Bitter Sweet

Every Autumn without fail
When I was fourteen years and more
We had to pick the apples in
And take them to the apple store.

> Placing the ladder against the tree,
> Reaching and stretching I gathered them in
> The ladder swayed – twigs would snap
> I'd end up performing a circus act.

Then a figure came on the scene
"Put them in basket stem side up
Treat them gently as you go
Please don't bruise them or they'll rot."

> Long stems, Bramleys, Golden Russets
> We picked apples all day long
> Queenies, Worcesters, Cox's Orange
> Bloody Butchers and Jonathons.

Of all the apples growing there
The Queenies were the very best.
Red right through, crisp and juicy
Far superior to the rest.

> Next came the bitter cider apples
> Lying scattered on the ground.
> Icy fingers – dirty picking
> All were thrown into a mound.

There they stayed till Whiteways came
Who loaded them upon their lorry.
And with the apple picking done
I couldn't say that I was sorry.

> Cider then went out of fashion
> Whiteways firm paid less and less
> So all the orchards were grubbed out
> But Devonshire cider remains the best.

A glass of scrumpy jets the blood stream
Tickles taste buds without doubt.
Let's all drink a toast to cider
A drink I wouldn't be without.

Cunning Bessie

Our father had a mangel cutter
Kept it in the great old barn.
Every day our farm boy Walter,
Ground the mangels in the maun,
Then he took them to the shippen
For the cows to feed upon.
One fine day we noticed Bessie
Sneaking in the barn-yard door
Craftily she reached the cutter
In her snout the handle bore.
Next she pushed it half way up
Brought it back towards the door.
A few odd mangels left in hopper
Splendid chippies on the floor.
From that day on we left her some
While we watched her grind away.
That old sow became our favourite
Entertained us every day.
For old Bessie had twelve piglets
Knew a thing or two I'd say.

The Dung Heap

Throughout the winter into spring
We watched the dung-heap getting higher
Horses, pigs and cows each day
Left their droppings in the way
Necessitating shovel and broom
Buckets of water for their rooms.
As time went on the heap piled up
Until they carted it away
When steam would rise up to the sky
And rats escape all through the day.
The dogs would bark and men would run
With heavy sticks to bash them one.
The stench so strong we held our noses
Not exactly Ashes of Roses
Next day the yard looked spick and span
Animals out for summer time.

Each spring the dung heap was carted to the fields and spread to fertilise the ground.

Counting the Bullocks

"Run down and count the bullocks
They're in the bottom meadow," said my father.
"You'll find sixteen – count them right."
"All right Dad," said I, and skipped off to find the gang,
"Come on you kids, we've got to count the bullocks,
I'll race you to the bottom,"
My voice echoing and re-echoing
Into the hills beyond.
Down the field we charged over the tufted grass
All glistening in the spring-filled air
Soon we were on the far side of the meadow
Faces burning, bodies tingling
Tearing the air as we flew pell-mell
To the far corner of the field.
Young bullocks grazing
Contentedly, on succulent, new-grown grass,
"I can only see fifteen," said brother Oliver
So we counted again three times over.....
And then the errant one appeared
Clambering from the ditch from where he drank,
How we breathed sighs of relief
Returning slowly.....
Through the gate.
"Let's go by the pond," said Anne,
Slowly, curiously exploring nooks and crannies
We reached the pond.
Where deep, black water, overhung by elders

Where a thousand grasses, reeds and rotten wood
Lay quietly, darkly menacing.....
Shaded by tangled brushwood.
Overcoming us,
Sending shivers down our spines,
Overhead birds were singing
Songs of early evening.
Shafts of sunlight penetrated the murky scene
Lighting up a coot's nest
Resting on a bed of reeds.
Where branch ends touch the water
Inside a clutch of eggs
Brown, with black spots, all nestling there together
In that splendid, rushy, root-filled nest
At branch end, safe from all intruders.
But I, in my fierce, young pride, coveted one such egg,
To take home to show my mother,
"I'm going to climb out on that branch!"
And with the same, with many a slip
And "Ohs" and "Ahs", from the other three
I finally reach the nest.....
Hanging on precariously.....
Broken twigs snapping, cracking
Leaves fluttering on to water's surface.
Reaching inside I took one spotted egg
And with fluttering heart made the perilous return
"Come on", I shouted, "Race you again"
Up a steep field we tore, lungs bursting, hearts racing
Hurtling through the garden gate

Into the farmhouse kitchen.
"Look what I've got", said I proudly,
Not noticing my father's presence
Who, on seeing the egg, turned fiercely,
"You naughty girl, how dare you take an **egg**
From a wild bird's nest.
Return it at once, and never do that again."
Tearfully I turned – joy turned to sorrow
And quietly crept from there,
To the bottom of the field again
Where, with downcast heart, and brothers watching
I slithered, and edged my way once more,
Along that knarled old trunk to branch end
Among the luxuriant growth of that weed-filled **pond**
Clutching a single ice-cold egg
With a heart as black as the very water
That lay beneath me.
Later that evening – Mum was darning – Dad was reading,
"Missus," he said,
"I went down the field to see the nest,
If I'd known where that egg had lain
I wouldn't have allowed her back
She could so easily have been drowned.

Brixham Meadow

Brixham Meadow!
Almost the last field on our farm.
Fascinating playground,
Nearly all year round.
Deep set winding streams
Where clear water flowed.
Complete with minnows
Slithering, slippery atoms –
We children – straw-corded jam jars – at the ready
Tried to catch them
As they darted with lightning speed
Streaking the sunlit water.
Miniature silver bullets
Out of sight in the twinkling of an eye.

Lying prone on mossy banks we sank our jars,
Quietly waiting.....
Suddenly – in they swam –
Swiftly we hauled them to the bank –
Stowed them safely –
While we played at crossing the flowing stream.

On great stepping stones
In shallower water.
Or the most daring
Vaulted across – where deep water swirled.
Where – falling meant a soaking,
And a telling off at home.
Happy care-free days
In childhood's fleeting Wonderland.

Wandering Alone in Spring

Often I wandered
Alone.....
Through the sidlings
Down to the meadow.
Where in Spring huge kingcups
Yellowing the marshy ground
Stood – in proud glory.
Beckoning me – enticing me –
To gather them.
Laughing at me,
Sure of their fastness
In that swampy bog.

Ragged robins
lured me.
Fluttering, swaying delicately
Where rushes and tall grasses
Waved their heads.
In homage to their Spring time beauty.
What happiness, peace and solace
The scene had brought.
To ease the pain in my sad heart.

The Travellers

Westcott Farm! Mecca for weary travellers,
Where the tea-pot was always ready and waiting,
And my mother's smiling face, welcoming all who came,
Neighbours, friends and travellers
From near and far.
"Sit down Mr Metherell, we're just about to eat,
We've rabbit pie today."
"Thank you, Mrs Carter," and putting his case aside
He joined us children in the settle
At our oblong oil-cloth covered table –
Soon we were tucking in
Finishing off the rice pudding
Followed by a cup of steaming tea.
"What have you brought us today?" said father,
Our Mr Metherell opened his vast and well-filled case.
And there – revealed – were flannelled shirts
Long pants, stiff, white celluloid collars, ties and socks,
Everything for the busy farmers
Who had no time – no desire –
to visit shops in Exeter city
In the High Street.
"It's time I ordered a new suit, Mother."
Straightway – out came a swotch of suitable materials.
Our eager, travelling salesman
Held several patterns in his thin, white hands,
And the bargaining began.

"Times are hard – we poor farmers,
Are at our wits end to scrape a living
It seems to me your prices are doubled
From what I paid for my last suit.
Let me see – must have been twenty years ago
And still as good as new but far too tight," he sighed,
An excellent salesman our Mr M –
"This suiting is top quality, Mr Carter,
Last you for another twenty."
And so – the deal was done,
Plus socks and a shirt or two –
Measurements taken and off he went
Into the greyness of the afternoon
From farm to farm,
The travelling salesman from the city.

A week or two later, Spargo came,
From Carters, the iron-mongers at Budleigh Salterton
Could it be accidental
That it was just on one o'clock and time to eat?
Smiling, friendly, kindly Spargo,
With his order book.
Miscellaneous Tools and everything for the farm
Were his trade –
Tools of all kinds, paring hooks – wood hooks –
Hay picks – manure forks.
Horse brushes – yard brushes – dairy brushes –
Hooks and eyes for hanging gates.
Nails for father to mend the doors – gates and fences.

Barbed wire – wire netting – fencing wire,
To keep the stock from straying.
Cord for tying corn – cord for thatching roofs and ricks,
Dairy utensils, disinfectant and strainer cloths.
All were his stock-in-trade –
To be delivered at a later date
By horse and wagon.
But Today!
Spargo came by bicycle
Hard slog through country lanes
Visiting all the farms,
In this particular neighbourhood.
"How are you off for paraffin – disinfectant, strainer cloths.
Grass seed – seed corn – seed potatoes?"
And so the list went on – and the book was closed,
"Thank you very much Mr Carter,"
After a good dinner and chat,
Off he went on his bicycle,
To the neighbouring farm.

Then came Veterinary supplies
Good old Mike Seward with his bag of tricks,
Joking and laughing with all and sundry,
Perfect apothecary for cure-all antidote –
"Day's Drenches," for sick animals,
No matter what the complaint –
"Day's Oil of the Night," excellent for man and beast,
Rheumatic pains and painful sprains –
"Salve," soothing amber unction,

Sore teats, painful udders, hard skin, chaps
Softened and as smooth as new again.
All of these wonderful remedies
Came under Mike's umbrella,
Even a cup of tea at the refreshment tent
A seat for weary farmers
At the Devon County Show.

Other travellers came and went,
Grocer, baker, butcher, gypsies,
A necessary part of country life
Bringing colour and change to Devon Days.

Miscellaneous

Life's Pattern

Two figures, arm in arm, stroll to the pond,
In the cool evening of an early Spring.
Lightly they tread, hoping to glimpse
The ageless ritual of leaping frogs –
Darting, quivering excitedly
Coldly aglow – siezed!
By the compelling urge
Of survival.

Bridging the decades – I recalled
When we strolled
Arm in Arm around a lake,
Twenty two miles by rugged mountains
And placid, gleaming water
Bathed in Summer's tender light.
As we, too, pledged our troth
Carelessly stepping into the unknown
Giving ourselves one to the other.

Joys and sorrows –
Come tumbling down the years.
United by a silken thread
So strong
It holds the fearsome weight
Of troubled times –
And binds us to the end of day.

*In memory of my husband Harry, and written for my Grandson Chris,
on his twenty fifth birthday. Seeing them by a Devon Garden Pond
evoked memories of long ago.*

In Memory of Fishleigh Gamble
Bishops Court 1984.

They're off – and away he thunders
Silver-grey streak barely touching the ground,
Pitting his speed against all the others
as he and his jockey take the first round.

In the background the green hills of Devon
Lightly veiled in cool winter mists
Bids the cool pale sun that is almost hidden
to temper and warm the winds icy gusts.

Trailers and vehicles of motley description
Stacked in the field there, row upon row
and motley the crowd, united in action
as from enclosure, to bookies, to racecourse they go.

Out on the field the third laps almost done,
Fishleigh Gamble's in front and picking up speed
With Pretty Polly Curling urging him on,
and the crowd begin shouting, "Come on" to their steeds.

But Fishleigh Gamble's already six lengths ahead,
and he takes the last fence at a cracking pace
Proud neck outstretched he's well in the lead
Proudly his owner leads him from the race.

Fishleigh Gamble met a tragic end the following year.

To The Sprinkler And Hose Brigade

Back in the Summer of '84
When it hadn't rained for three months or more
To and fro to the garden we went
With the washing-up water from the sink
We could hardly ask for our money back
If the flowers all shrivelled and the leaves went slack
Having paid a tidy sum at the nursery
We couldn't see our plants go thirsty
When the hose-pipe ban was passed by law –
So in spite of aching legs and all
For days and weeks my partner and me
Hunked buckets of water to flowers and trees
Ah me, it's November 23rd!
And if I speak I can hardly be heard
For a gale is blowing and its chucking it down
Our trees are almost bent to the ground
While from rivers and streams and sundry places
A million gallons of water races
Hell bent it surges to the ocean
To be lost in the depths – O what a notion!
And now my thoughts to the Summer turn
And I picture ourselves – bucket in hand
With the washing-up water all covered in spume
Trying to keep old Britain in Bloom.....
When for weeks and months my partner and me
Hunked buckets and buckets to flowers and trees.....
I advise all you gardeners who might read these lines
To build up your strength in Winter time
For just mark my words – there's lean times ahead
When the sprinklers and hoses are locked in the shed

Rockabye Blues

Ten years ago at Rockabye
All was quiet and still
So we bought us a barn conversion
Just at the foot of the hill

Nearby the river ran sweetly
And the water was crystal clear
We thought it would last forever
How foolish we were then my dear!

For the once quiet village is teeming
With commuters from near and far
Scurrying like rats from their bolt-holes
In their latest high-tech cars

And the once quiet by-ways are straightened
To adjust to the daily round
So we have to leave good and early
To park our car in the town

For the parish is full of us townies
Who hoped to get away from it all
Holed up in mortgaged houses
Longing for an interest fall

Now it's the same in the village
As it was for us back in town
It seems that we've come full circle
For where is the peace that we'd found?

Exeter – Exeter Airport

Market Day

After the usual upheaval Joey turned left
Into the yard of the White Hart.
Parking for ponies –
Meeting place for farmers.
After the cattle market.
Bread and cheese – pints of beer –
Cattle talk – lewd jokes – latest scandal
Men's talk.
While we women shopped
Banked the week's takings
Exchanging pleasantries with Miss Wilson.
"Such a charming woman", said mum,
As we crossed the street to Dellers.
"We'll have a pot of tea and cakes".
Climbing the steep steps
Of this imposing restaurant.
I clung to her.
We found a table.....
Ordered a pot of tea – scrumptious cakes,
"Mum, look at the people dancing!"
Dance band – black suited musicians
Churning out light music –
Quick steps – foxtrots – waltz and tango
Dancers, sedately turning,
"Tea for two and two for tea."
"Do you know how to dance?" I asked.
"I used to go to the ball", she replied wistfully.
"But now there isn't time."
Wonderful Dellers – On three levels,

Balconies overlooking the dance floor
Brilliant murals, exotic scenes
Colourful, warm and vibrant
Tables strategically placed
For unlimited view of the dance floor,
Burnished parquet
Perfect get away.
From stressful farm or business
In the heart of Exeter City.

Dellers received a direct hit during the Exeter blitz.

Saturday Night

Saturday Night!
Exeter City – pulsating with life.
Mums – Dads and children, miscellaneous crowds
Converging on City Centre – just to window shop.
Be part of the scene – Or go to the cinema.
Brightly lit streets – Bobby's Arcade, Colsons, Dellers or Berni's
Crowds thronging public places
Saturday night! when all the world converged
Into the golden heart.....
At the same time watching pennies in cash-short times.
What did it matter? When all were imbued
By a sense of belonging – mutual satisfaction.
Small pleasures in life? Innocent enjoyment
Of simple things.
Like queuing for the pictures
Hundreds of us in snake-like lines patiently waiting –
Winter – stamping feet – bitter cold weather
Huddled together –
Would we make it in time for the beginning?
In time for the organ at the Savoy?
Or Clark Gable at the Gaumont?
Good nature prevailed
Wasn't it our night off?

Inside.....
A thick pall of cigarette smoke,
Billowed, rising cloud-like to the ceiling

IN FLAMES A MiLLION DREAMS

No feeling of fear in those care-free days
As we sat – close – holding hands
While the old films rolled.

Into the night air.
Fish and chips wrapped in newspaper,
Tramping narrow streets
Or – special treat – up winding, narrow stairways
Sitting at tables.
Chatting – joking – care-free youth, untried in life's battle
Afire – burning for the future –
Saturday Fever held us in its grip.

Epilogue

Bombs rained down on Exeter City
Old shops – winding stairways,
Buildings – Cathedral – Dellers.
Consumed by flames.
In flames a million dreams –
Lost generations, missed openings, closed aspirations
As we fought for our lives in those far-off times.
What price glory? In the burning of the cities?
Wasted lives.
Sacrifice – a task to be done
For a future when we'd be free?

Memories of Exeter Airport – World War II

War Time! Once peaceful fields
Clothed in armour.
Dotted with Hurricanes and Spitfires
Countering enemy invasion.
Chasing Dorniers from Portland to Dartmouth.
Brave airmen risking life and limb
Fully supported by ground crew.
Battle of Britain Heroes!
Holding the life-line of our dear Land.

We played a part in our small way.
Running a milk round in the city.
Showing passes
At the airport sentry posts
Allowing us through the lanes.
Forbidden to most civilians.
Lanes, where once we walked
Observing nature's labour.
Wild strawberries, cherries, gleaming blackberry.
Field mice scampering in periwinkle terraces –
Overlooking ditches, where stickle-backs skulked,
Near blue forget-me-nots, snap jacks, yellow celandine.
Hap-hazard bounty – soon to be destroyed,
When Tar-Mac would be King.

Germans bombed and strafed the airport
Machine gunning up, down and across,
Debris strewing the ground
Scattering billets, blankets, bedding in trees.
No-where to sleep for airmen.
But villagers rose to the occasion.
Willingly took them in.
Seventeen Polish Airmen billeted at home.
And others – round a-bout.
Friendly, polite, refugees from a far off land,
Holding the door open for our mother,
Closing it carefully – unheard of attention.
"Would you leave our milk – a couple of days or so?
We prefer to drink it sour?"
So each day – bowls of sour milk
Waited their return from the airport
Long before Yoghurt arrived here – strange to us
Soon the Polish airmen joined in family life.
Helping here and there in spare time.
Socialising – pictures at the camp,
Dancing – how they danced!

Epilogue
Raids – bombing of towns and cities –
Sinking of warships – and little boats
Continued relentlessly
Airport personnel prepared for final invasion
In buoyant mood, the people waited –
Prepared and unafraid.

Ladram Bay, Otterton
The Seagull

Seagull where are you flying today?
What makes you screech so and call?
What did you see out there on the ocean?
Come back and tell me all.

Shipwrecks and storms and fear and death,
Darkness and sorrow and tears.
What did you see out there on the ocean?
Come back and tell me, dear.

Beaches and warmth and mermaids and love,
Islands and palms and balmy seas.
What did you see out there on the ocean?
Come back and tell me please.

Skiers and divers and swimmers I saw,
Fishermen too, a tale without end,
That's what I saw out there on the ocean,
And I've come back to tell you my friend.

In Memory of the Elm Trees at Ladram Bay

Along the slip-way leading to the beach
A gracious line of elm trees stand,
Proudly – tall and straight...
Leafy heads reaching to the sky.
People come and go in the wakening year
When palest greens gloss branch and twig
Glad – that once again a new beginning
Will wipe away the sorrows of the past.

Summers children – laughing, playing, climbing
Scale the banks where the elm trees stand
While down the path come scores of trippers
Out for the day – or simply to admire the view.

When long, grey shadows cross the silvered grass
Shimmering spiders' webs glisten everywhere
For Autumn's treasure trove has burst upon the scene
Carelessly flinging its golden offerings –
Communion of leaves with the waiting earth.

Then winter's stormy winds and cleansing frosts
On cold, dark days descend upon the scene
Silhouetting trees against the leaden skies,
Like magic filigree, delicately traced
And there they rest – waiting for renaissance
When palest green will gloss again their twigs
And other children come to laugh and play
Beneath their shade – while other people wander up and down
Each bent upon the business of the day.

Hedge Massacre Barr Lane 1984

Straddling High Peak
Straight-growing conifers and larches
are reaching for the sky
Arching and re-arching by woodland paths
Rising tall from scrub-carpeted ground
In the Spring filled wood.

In the lane below
The chain-saw's screech splits the ear in two
Echoing and re-echoing through waving tree-tops
Sounding and resounding in the valley below
while small woodland creatures take to flight
From hedge to field, to wood or cliff top.

Weep now for trampled blue-bells
Or the last few primroses scenting the morning air
Lost promise of filberts in the Autumn.....
Weep for what has been – then turn your thoughts away
To matters far more pressing
Than passing thoughts of wild things in the Spring

This hedge is almost restored to its former beauty.

Barton Days – Childhood Recalled

Otterton Barton, a beautiful Devonshire farm, is situated on top of the hill adjoining Otterton Church. The "Childhood Recalled", is based on the many times I stayed with my grandparents, Mr and Mrs Sydenham Cater, who farmed there, with their sons, for many years. The farm belongs to Lord Clinton and later became part of Bicton Agricultural College. Sadly, the lovely, old long house and magnificent buildings seem likely to be turned into a building complex.

In days past the meadows contained an enormous variety of wild flowers while two rows of poplar trees divided the fields which are now turned into one. Salmon and trout were plentiful, while the river was kept in bounds by various farmers, whose duty it was to lay elm logs along the banks. Rowan bushes and willow were planted extensively, helping to contain them and prevented the erosion that we see there today. Kingfishers, butterflies and dragon flies completed the scene, surely one of the most beautiful spots to be seen in the British Isles.

Barton Days

"Planning permission has been granted"
My thoughts turn to the dear, old Barton
Of my early days
And my corner bedroom – right next to the Church
Where I lay – a child
Listening to the bells, the thud of the ropes
As peal after peal rang out across the valley –
Listening –
Listening to the changes – each following each
In perfect unison.
How wonderful to lie there!
Cosy and warm – tucked up in lavender – scented sheets
In my feather bed.
Cacophony of sound – cocks crowing,
The early stir of the milkers,
Mooing of cows,
All in glorious profusion.
Early dawn on Sunday morning.
And then – later with my Aunts
Walking sedately to Church
Where I sat – in appointed seat.
Stiff as a ram-rod – thoughts running riot.

Of clear trout-filled water,
The Otter!
Rippling and coursing to the sea
Large, blue dragonflies

Glinting in the sunlight.
Or the rows of poplars
Sentinels – dividing the herb-filled meadows
Of my wonder world.
Sometimes – taking my life in hand
I walked across the weir
Sure-footed in the river from the mill
From stepping stone to stepping stone.
Gazing into the murky depths
Tingling body – half scared – half filled
With the glory of it all.
Happy childhood days –
As memory after memory impinges on my mind
Me – standing in the yard:
Watching the great horses,
Manes, tails, brushed and shining – a ribbon here and there,
Harness all aglow
Led by the ploughmen
To the fields of Home Down.
My uncles, open-necked flannelled shirts,
Sleeves rolled to the elbows
Returning dead on time,
To lunch in the wood-scented kitchen
Where great hams hung
In the sombre smoke-filled recess
Of the huge, old fireplace,
Bread oven at side.
While over the fire
Kettles on bar crooks sang –

And the saucepans steamed on the brandice
Black as the witches' cauldron,
Waiting the attention of the women folk.
And always the cider!
Freshly drawn –
The cool, fusty, damp, old cellar
In wooden hogs-head neatly stacked.
Dynamite to the uninitiated!
Golden – sparkling – throat tickling
Barton champagne.
Sunday was a special day
Six days shalt thou labour!
Worship and prayers
Joints at the bakery
Perfectly cooked and sizzling
Visiting farmers and their wives
Left their horses and traps
In the Barton yard,
Came, after Church, for drinks and gossip.
And then:

In our dining room the table was set
for Sunday lunch,
Where, in unaccustomed black.
Our family and may-be friends
Gathered –
A feast!
Huge, succulent, roast beef
By bone-handled, carving knife

Lay ready for Granddad
Hot, seasonal vegetables, freshly gathered
Waited in gleaming dishes, for hungry people
On the old-fashioned, mahogany sideboard.
Stood the junket – topped with slivers
of Devonshire cream.
Or in their time – strawberries
from Uncle Jim's garden,
Or apple tart and cream
On the lengthy, snow-white table cloth
Blue and white table-ware, gleaming silver –
And always the cider!
And I – an inquisitive, observant child –
Let my thoughts wander –
Half listening to farm talk
Weather – crops – the price of livestock
.....While I dreamt of picnics
By the Otter –
Maybe in primrose time.....
Or it could be bluebells
Lining the river bank.
And always the kingfishers
Flashing – brilliant blue and red
Jewelling the river.
Otterton Barton!
How I adored you!
You brought colour to my young life
You filled me with happy memories
Of a gentler past – those happy, halcyon days

Soon to disappear into time – swallowing
Months and years.....
That mould the history of life.

The village street comes into view
Quiet and peaceful,
Where twice a day the dairy cows
Plodded slowly from field to shippon!
Where horses were brought to the warm and acrid smithy
To be fitted with brand new shoes.
Where Mr Fayter, the blacksmith, plied his trade.
Freeman and Genge!
In their spice-scented grocers' emporium
A veritable treasure trove for all,
Miss Baker, cutting down Aunty's dresses
For me, a country girl from a large family
Make do and mend.....
The market – once a week.
All hustle and bustle,
And the mill.
And always the swirling water
Racing through the leat!
Where the great wheel turned,
Husks and corn and dust, mingled and intermingled
Clouding walls and men
Where sacks were filled – bought and sold
A never-ending harvest
Of grain and beast, in sweltering heat
Or griping cold.

Enacting the age-old farming story.

My thoughts turn!
I see a frightened child
Filled with heart-stopping fear
A huge wing-flapping gander
Screeching, chased me, wings whirring
Pandemonium complete.

Dogs barking, hens squawking, feathers flying
While gleenies took to flight
Somehow I made it to the gate
Hurling myself through the open door
To the safety of the kitchen.
And the three-legged stool in the chimney corner
Consoled by warmth and loving Aunt.
"Run down and pick up the eggs", she said
Handing me a basket
And I, forgetting fear, ran through the wicket gate
Into the kitchen garden.
Where peaches and nectarines
Hung golden on the walls
Into the paddock below
There – in the great, old barn
Were warm, brown eggs
In nooks and corners
Wispy feathers still clinging.
I searched them out
Amid the squawking hens

And brought them to my dear, Aunt Mabel
Who took them to our cream-filled dairy
Placed them in a wicker basket
Waiting collection by the egg man.

Back in the dear, old house
There was always -
The wood-scented cosiness.
Permeating kitchen and corridors
As we click-clacked
Over the yellow-bricked floor
Or I tip-toed into Grandma's room.
Glorious times when I stayed at the Barton
Often when a new baby arrived
And I was packed off out of the way.....
My luck was in for those days remain
A clear oasis in my long and varied life.